Indoor Grilling

Recipes Featured on TV
by Meriel Bradley

Indoor Grilling

Website: www.MerielBradley.com
Copyright © 2002 by Emmadee Communications Inc.
Published by EXI International Inc.

Printed and bound
in Canada

Forward

GRILLING is fast becoming one of the most popular ways to cook. Why? Because it offers us a quick way to produce tempting, flavorful meals.

The recipes that follow are both easy to prepare, and delicious to eat - helping you produce fast food, truly at its best.

I've designed the recipes specifically for use on indoor electric grills, but they can easily be adapted for use on any outdoor barbecue.

Follow the Quick Tips and learn how to maximize your time in the kitchen. With a little planning, your freezer will soon become stocked with healthy, home-made frozen meals you can easily pull out and grill when time is short.

INDOOR GRILLING will help you will discover a whole new world of food. Enjoy!

Meriel Bradley

Indoor Grilling

Website: www.MerielBradley.com

VISIT WWW.MERIELBRADLEY.COM TO:

- Send your comments
- Submit recipes, tips and ideas for inclusion in upcoming books and on TV
- Preview future volumes in the Meriel Bradley cookbook series

NOTES ON COOKING TIMES

Cooking times given are approximate only. Please follow the directions given in the instruction manual for your own model and make of grill.

A meat or food thermometer can be used to measure the internal temperature of meats and ensure your food is properly cooked.

Contents

Seafood   8

Poultry 24

Beef 42

Pork 58

Vegetables 72

Desserts 88

Snacks 100

Sandwiches 104

New from Meriel 121

Index 126

Seafood

Stuffed Trout

4 large trout fillets with
   the skin on
2 tablespoons butter
1 small onion diced and
   seasoned with salt
   and pepper
2 cups soft breadcrumbs
1½ cups chopped mushrooms

1 Pre-heat grill.

2 Wash trout and pat dry.

3 Heat butter in a small pan, add diced onion and simmer until tender.

4 Mix breadcrumbs, parsley and chopped mushrooms in a small bowl. Add onions, mix well.

5 Divide the stuffing and spread over one half of each trout fillet. Fold fillets over and secure with wooden cocktail sticks.

6 Place trout fillets on the grill and cook for 10-12 minutes or until done.

QUICK TIP

For a quick future meal, prepare additional stuffed fillets with previously unfrozen trout, then freeze (uncooked). To cook, place fillets on the grill after defrosting and cook as in direction 6.

Serves: 4

Preparation time: 15 minutes

Indoor Grilling by Meriel Bradley :: www.MerielBradley.com

Thyme for Trout

2 large trout filleted
4 tablespoons butter
$\frac{1}{4}$ cup cooking sherry or dry
   white wine
$\frac{1}{2}$ tablespoon dried thyme
Fresh ground salt and pepper
   to taste

1 Pre-heat grill.

2 Wash trout fillets and pat dry.

3 In a small bowl mix butter, cooking sherry, dried thyme and fresh ground salt and pepper together to form a paste.

4 Spread over the trout fillets and fold in half.

5 Place trout fillets on the grill with the fold of the fish on the lower end of the grill's slope and cook for 7 - 8 minutes or until done.

Serves: 2 - 4

Preparation time: 10 minutes

Haddock with Mustard & Dill

2 large haddock fillets
1 cup natural set yogurt
½ cup chopped fresh dill
1 tablespoon mustard
Fresh ground salt and pepper
    to taste

1. Wash haddock fillets and pat dry.

2. Mix yogurt, dill, mustard and fresh ground salt & pepper together.

3. Pour mixture over fish fillets and allow to marinate for at least 1 hour before cooking.

4. Pre-heat grill.

5. Place the fish on the grill and cook for 5 - 6 minutes or until done.

Serves: 2 - 4

Preparation time: 10 minutes

Indoor Grilling by Meriel Bradley :: www.MerielBradley.com

Seafood Stir Fry

¹/₂ purple onion sliced
¹/₂ green pepper sliced
¹/₂ red pepper sliced
1 cup bamboo shoots
¹/₂ cup water chestnuts
¹/₂ cup sliced mushrooms
1 cup baby corn chopped
1 cup shrimp peeled and
   de-veined
¹/₂ cup scallops
2 tablespoons soy sauce
1 teaspoon brown sugar
¹/₂ teaspoon chopped fresh
   ginger
Fresh ground salt & pepper
   to taste
¹/₃ cup roasted salted
   cashew nuts

1 Pre-heat grill.

2 Place all the ingredients except cashew nuts in a bowl and mix well.

3 Place the mix on the grill and cook for 5 - 6 minutes or until done.

4 Stir in cashews just before serving.

Serves: 4

Preparation time: 15 minutes

Spicy Shrimp

1½ pounds shrimp peeled
   and de-veined
½ cup coconut milk
Juice from ½ lime
¼ teaspoon fish sauce
¼ teaspoon red curry paste
   (more if you like it spicy)
¼ teaspoon salt

1 Mix coconut milk, lime juice, fish sauce, red curry paste and salt together.

2 Pour over shrimp, mix well and allow to marinate for at least 1 hour before cooking.

3 Pre-heat grill.

4 Place the shrimp on the grill and cook for 5 - 6 minutes or until done.

5 This is good served with peanut satay sauce, available in your grocery store.

Serves: 4

Preparation time: 10 minutes

Indoor Grilling by Meriel Bradley :: www.MerielBradley.com

Fish Cakes

1 tin salmon, drained
   (approx. 7.5 oz.)
1 pound potatoes mashed
   with $1/2$ tablespoon butter
   and 2 tablespoons milk
4 tablespoons fresh parsley
   chopped
2 scallions chopped
Salt and pepper to taste

1 Mix all ingredients together and form into flat cakes.

2 Place in refrigerator and allow to cool.

3 Brush grill with a little oil and pre-heat.

4 Place fish cakes on the grill and cook for 7 - 8 minutes or until done.

QUICK TIP

The next time you make mashed potatoes, make extra so you can make a batch of these delicious fish cakes the next day.

Makes: 8 cakes

Preparation time: 10 - 15 minutes

Herb Salmon with Cream Sauce

1 pound salmon fillets, about
    1 inch thick
1 garlic clove, crushed
3 tablespoons fresh tarragon
3 tablespoons fresh parsley
4 tablespoons yogurt
2 tablespoons butter
1 tablespoon lemon juice
Fresh ground salt and pepper
    to taste

1 Pre-heat grill.

2 Cut salmon into pieces 2" wide across their width.

3 Chop herbs, scatter on a plate & roll salmon pieces in them, pressing down so they adhere to the fish. Season well.

4 Place salmon on the grill and cook 4 - 5 minutes.

5 While salmon is cooking, melt butter in a shallow pan over medium heat & add garlic.

6 When butter starts to bubble, stir in yogurt and leave to melt into butter. Season and add lemon juice.

7 Remove salmon from the grill, pour sauce over and serve.

Serves: 2 - 3

Preparation time: 15 minutes

Indoor Grilling by Meriel Bradley :: www.MerielBradley.com

Mediterranean Seafood Kebabs

32 large shrimp peeled
32 cherry tomatoes
32 pearl onions peeled
Juice and zest of 1 lemon
2 tablespoons olive oil
$^1/_2$ tablespoon dried oregano
Fresh ground salt and pepper
 to taste

1 Soak 8 bamboo skewers in water for $^1/_2$ an hour.

2 Thread on, 4 shrimp, 4 tomatoes and 4 pearl onions per skewer.

3 Mix the seasonings, and pour over the skewers.

4 Leave to marinate for $^1/_2$ an hour.

5 Pre-heat grill.

6 Place skewers on the grill and cook for 5 - 6 minutes or until done.

Serves: 2 - 4

Preparation time: 15 minutes

Scallop Kebabs

1 pound large scallops
4 tablespoons oyster sauce
1 tablespoon soy sauce
1 teaspoon sesame oil
1 clove garlic crushed

1 Soak 8 bamboo skewers in water for $1/2$ an hour.

2 Mix the scallops with all the other ingredients and allow to marinate for $1/2$ an hour.

3 Pre-heat grill.

4 Thread the scallops onto the skewers.

5 Place skewers on the grill and cook for 5 - 6 minutes or until done.

Serves: 2 - 4

Preparation time: 10 minutes

Indoor Grilling by Meriel Bradley :: www.MerielBradley.com

Herb Salmon Steaks

4 salmon fillets
$\frac{1}{2}$ cup dry white wine
2 tablespoons olive oil
$\frac{1}{2}$ tablespoon fresh chopped
thyme
$\frac{1}{2}$ tablespoon fresh chopped
parsley
$\frac{1}{2}$ tablespoon fresh chopped
coriander
Fresh ground salt and pepper
to taste

1 Mix the marinade ingredients together and add salmon, coating well.

2 Allow to marinate for $\frac{1}{2}$ an hour.

3 Pre-heat the grill.

4 Place salmon on the grill and cook for 5 - 6 minutes or until done.

Serves: 4

Preparation time: 10 minutes

Shrimp Toast

4 slices sliced white bread
1 cup chopped cooked
    shrimp
2 scallions finely minced
1 egg white
2 tablespoons dry white
    wine
1 tablespoon sesame seeds
Butter for bread

1 Pre-heat grill.

2 Butter the bread slices on one side and sprinkle with sesame seeds.

3 Pour the wine over the shrimp.

4 Beat the egg white until stiff.

5 Fold in shrimp & scallions.

6 Divide the mixture in half and spread over the unbuttered side of 2 bread slices.

7 Place the remaining bread slices on top, butter-side up, completing the sandwiches butter-side out.

8 Place sandwiches on the grill and cook for 4 minutes or until done.

Serves: 2

Preparation time: 10 minutes

Indoor Grilling by Meriel Bradley :: www.MerielBradley.com

Crab Stuffed Salmon Wheels

2 large skinless salmon fillets
1 cup ricotta cheese
1 cup crab meat
1 cup breadcrumbs
$1/2$ cup chopped roasted
  red peppers (bottled
  works well)
1 tablespoon dried Italian
  herb seasoning
Fresh ground salt and pepper
  to taste

1 In a bowl combine all ingredients except salmon.

2 Spread the mixture evenly over the salmon fillets.

3 Roll up jelly-roll style.

4 Pre-heat grill.

5 With a sharp knife cut 1 inch slices along the length of the rolled up salmon.

6 Place salmon slices on the grill and cook for 4 minutes or until done.

QUICK TIP

For improved flavor, try making your own breadcrumbs from scratch. Use a food processor or blender and follow the manufactures instructions. Fresh bread crumbs freeze well, so make a big batch and freeze them in a bag.

Serves: 4 - 6

Preparation time: 15 minutes

Stuffed Orange Roughy

4 orange roughy fillets
1 tablespoon butter
$\frac{1}{2}$ onion finely diced
$\frac{1}{2}$ red pepper finely diced
$\frac{1}{2}$ cup cooked rice
$\frac{1}{2}$ cup corn
1 teaspoon dried Italian herb
   seasoning
Fresh ground salt and pepper
   to taste

1 Very carefully make a slit along the length of each fish fillet to make a pocket.

2 Pre-heat the grill.

3 Melt butter in a pan and add onions and peppers. Cook for 2 or 3 minutes.

4 In a bowl mix rice, corn and seasonings.

5 Add onions and peppers and mix well.

6 Stuff each fish fillet carefully with the filling.

7 Place fish on the grill and cook for 5 - 6 minutes or until done.

Serves: 4

Preparation time: 15 minutes

Indoor Grilling by Meriel Bradley :: www.MerielBradley.com

Red Snapper
with Lime

2 large red snapper fillets
Zest and juice of 1 lime
1 tablespoon dried cajun
    seasoning

1 Marinate red snapper in seasonings for $1/2$ an hour.

2 Pre-heat grill.

3 Place fish on the grill and cook for 5 - 6 minutes or until done.

Serves: 2 - 4

Preparation time: 5 minutes

Maple Mustard Glazed Salmon

4 small salmon fillets
6 tablespoons maple syrup
$\frac{1}{2}$ tablespoon mustard seeds
1 tablespoon mustard
$\frac{1}{2}$ teaspoon salt
Juice of $\frac{1}{2}$ a lemon

1. Mix marinade ingredients together and add fish, coating well.

2. Allow to marinate for $\frac{1}{2}$ an hour.

3. Pre-heat grill.

4. Place fish on the grill and cook for 5 - 6 minutes or until done.

QUICK TIP

Grilling is quick! Be sure not to overcook your foods or they may end up dry and tough.

Serves: 4

Preparation time: 5 minutes

Indoor Grilling by Meriel Bradley :: www.MerielBradley.com

Poultry

Raspberry Chicken

4 boneless chicken breasts
4 tablespoons natural, plain
   yogurt
2 tablespoons corn oil
1 clove minced garlic
2 tablespoons raspberry
   vinegar
Fresh ground salt and pepper
   to taste

① Mix marinade ingredients together and add chicken, coating well.

② Allow to marinate in the refrigerator for ½ an hour.

③ Pre-heat grill.

④ Place chicken on the grill and cook for 5 - 6 minutes or until done.

⑤ Serve with cranberry jelly.

> **QUICK TIP**
>
> *Always pre-heat your grill —
> this will ensure your foods
> are instantly sealed, locking
> in all the flavor and juices.*

Serves: 4

Preparation time: 5 minutes

Aromatic Chicken Skewers

1 pound chicken cubed
   (approx. 4 boneless
   chicken breasts)
1 cup coconut milk
1 tablespoon ground cumin
Juice and zest from $\frac{1}{2}$ lime
1 teaspoon salt

1 Mix marinade ingredients together and add chicken, coating well.

2 Allow to marinate in the refrigerator for $\frac{1}{2}$ an hour.

3 Soak 8 bamboo skewers in water for $\frac{1}{2}$ an hour.

4 Pre-heat grill.

5 Thread chicken onto skewers.

6 Place chicken skewers on the grill and cook for 4 - 5 minutes or until done.

7 Serve with satay peanut sauce, available in your grocery store.

Serves: 4

Preparation time: 5 minutes

Orange Ginger Chicken

4 boneless chicken breasts
$1/3$ cup orange juice
$1/3$ cup orange marmalade
1 teaspoon ground ginger
$1/4$ teaspoon salt

1 Mix marinade ingredients together and add chicken, coating well.

2 Allow to marinate for $1/2$ an hour.

3 Pre-heat grill.

4 Place chicken on the grill and cook for 5 - 6 minutes or until done.

Serves: 4

Preparation time: 5 minutes

Lime Butter Chicken

4 boneless chicken breasts
4 tablespoons melted butter
Zest and juice of 1 lime
1 tablespoon sugar
$1/4$ teaspoon salt

1 Pre-heat grill.

2 Mix melted butter, lime zest and salt together. Allow to cool before adding chicken if not cooking right away.

3 Add chicken breasts, coat well.

4 Allow to stand until butter starts to set around the chicken (approx. 5 minutes).

5 Place chicken on the grill and cook for 5 - 6 minutes or until done.

QUICK TIP

If using a sloped grill, place vegetables at the high end of the grill and meats at the low end. This will allow the vegetable juices to roll down into the meats, while the meat fats roll into the drip tray without affecting the vegetables.

Serves: 4

Preparation time: 10 minutes

Spiced Chicken

4 boneless chicken breasts
4 tablespoons melted butter
1 teaspoon ground cumin
1 teaspoon ground coriander
$1/4$ teaspoon salt
1 pinch chili powder or
   to taste

1 Pre-heat grill.

2 Mix spices together with the butter and salt. Allow to cool before adding chicken if not cooking right away.

3 Add chicken breasts, coat well.

4 Allow to stand for 5 minutes until butter starts to set around the chicken.

5 Place chicken on the grill and cook for 5 - 6 minutes or until done.

Serves: 4

Preparation time: 10 minutes

Indoor Grilling by Meriel Bradley :: www.MerielBradley.com

Chicken with Sweet Orange

4 boneless chicken breasts
$1/2$ cup orange juice
2 tablespoons butter
1 tablespoon brown sugar
$1/4$ teaspoon paprika
$1/4$ teaspoon ground ginger
$1/4$ teaspoon salt

1 Pre-heat grill.

2 Mix the melted butter with all other ingredients except the chicken. Allow to cool before adding the chicken if not cooking right away.

3 Add chicken breasts, coat well.

4 Allow to stand for 5 minutes until butter starts to set around the chicken.

5 Place chicken on the grill and cook for 5 - 6 minutes or until done.

Serves: 4

Preparation time: 10 minutes

Chicken with Garlic, Lemon & Herbs

4 boneless chicken breasts
$1/4$ cup fresh chopped parsley
1 teaspoon dried Italian herb
   seasoning
2 cloves garlic chopped
Juice of 1 lemon
1 tablespoon olive oil
Fresh ground salt and pepper
   to taste

1 Mix marinade ingredients together and add chicken, coating well.

2 Allow to marinate for $1/2$ an hour.

3 Pre-heat grill.

4 Place chicken on the grill and cook for 5 - 6 minutes or until done.

Serves: 4

Preparation time: 5 minutes

Indoor Grilling by Meriel Bradley :: www.MerielBradley.com

Chicken Strips

4 chicken breasts
2 eggs beaten
$1/2$ cup cornstarch
2 cups breadcrumbs mixed
    with 4 tablespoons oil
Juice of 1 lime

1. Cut each breast into 4 strips pieces.

2. Marinate in lime juice for $1/2$ hour.

3. Place cornstarch in a bag and add chicken. Shake to cover each piece of chicken with the cornstarch.

4. Dip each piece of chicken into beaten egg, then roll in breadcrumbs.

5. Repeat with each piece of chicken.

6. Pre-heat grill.

7. Place chicken strips on the grill and cook for 6 - 7 minutes or until done (you may need to turn them while cooking).

Makes: 16 strips

Preparation time: 20 minutes

Chicken Wings

24 chicken wings
2 cloves minced garlic
1 tablespoon olive oil
$\frac{1}{2}$ cup tomato paste
$\frac{1}{2}$ cup water
1 tablespoon brown sugar
1 tablespoon Balsamic
   vinegar
$\frac{1}{2}$ tablespoon French style
   mustard
2 teaspoons paprika
Chili powder to taste
Salt and pepper to taste

QUICK TIP
Never use metal utensils on a non-stick grilling surface – use plastic or wooden utensils only.

1. Mix all ingredients except the chicken wings together.

2. Pour over the wings and allow to marinade for at least 2 hours.

3. Pre-heat grill.

4. Place wings on the grill and cook for 10 - 12 minutes or until done.

Serves: 4 - 6

Preparation time: 10 minutes

Whole Split Chicken

1 chicken split along the breast bone and flattened (get your butcher to do this making sure the joints are pulled apart to lie flat on the grill)
4 tablespoons olive oil
1 teaspoon salt
1 teaspoon garlic powder
10 fresh rosemary leaves

1. Mix all ingredients together except the chicken.

2. Rub into chicken.

3. Allow to marinade at least 2 hours before grilling.

4. Pre-heat grill.

5. Place chicken on the grill and cook for 25 - 35 minutes or until done, turning several times during cooking.

Makes: 1 chicken

Preparation time: 10 minutes

Chicken Fajitas

½ pound chicken strips in
   a bowl with 2 tablespoons
   soy sauce
1 cup red/yellow/green
   pepper slices
⅓ cup grated cheese
2 tortillas

1. Place chicken at the low end and peppers at the high end of the grill and cook for 4 - 5 minutes or until the chicken is done.

2. Remove chicken and peppers from grill.

3. Place tortillas on the grill and cook for 1 minute.

4. Place tortillas on a plate, add chicken and peppers, sprinkle with cheese, roll up and enjoy!

Serves: 1 - 2 \◎ℍ

Preparation time: 10 minutes ↻

Rosemary Butter Stuffed Chicken Thighs

4 chicken thighs de-boned
(get your butcher to do
this for you)
1 cup breadcrumbs
1 medium onion diced
2 tablespoons butter
1 tablespoon fresh chopped
rosemary
4 tablespoon fresh chopped
parsley
Fresh ground salt and pepper
to taste

1. In a small pan, heat the butter, add diced onion and simmer until tender.

2. Combine the remaining stuffing ingredients and add cooked onions and butter. Allow to cool before stuffing chicken if not cooking right away.

3. Pre-heat grill.

4. Divide the stuffing mix between each chicken thigh.

5. Fold over and secure with wooden cocktail sticks.

6. Place chicken on the grill and cook for 7 - 8 minutes or until done.

Serves: 2 - 4

Preparation time: 15 minutes

Turkey Burgers

1 pound ground turkey
1 onion chopped
1 apple peeled and grated
1 clove minced garlic
1 teaspoon dried Italian herb
   seasoning
$1/2$ cup oats
$1/2$ teaspoon salt
Pepper to taste

1 Combine all ingredients.

2 Shape into four $1/2$ inch thick patties.

3 Pre-heat grill.

4 Place turkey burgers on the grill and cook 10 - 12 minutes or until done.

Serves: 2 - 4

Preparation time: 10 minutes

Indoor Grilling by Meriel Bradley :: www.MerielBradley.com

Rosemary Lemon Chicken

4 chicken breasts
1 tablespoon olive oil
Zest and juice of $1/2$ lemon
1 clove minced garlic
1 teaspoon paprika
10 fresh rosemary leaves
$1/4$ teaspoon salt

1 Mix all marinade ingredients together.

2 Add chicken breasts and allow to marinade for a minimum of 2 hours.

3 Pre-heat grill.

4 Place chicken on the grill and cook for 5 - 6 minutes or until done.

QUICK TIP
Marinate foods in a refrigerator — not at room temperature.

Serves: 4

Preparation time: 5 minutes

Chicken Cordon Bleu

4 chicken breasts
4 slices ham
4 slices Swiss cheese
3 tablespoons cornstarch
2 eggs beaten
2 cups breadcrumbs mixed
    with 4 tablespoons oil

1 Slit chicken breasts lengthwise to form a pocket.

2 Place one slice of ham and one slice of cheese into each breast.

3 Pre heat grill.

4 Dip each breast into cornstarch, then egg, and then roll in breadcrumbs.

5 Place chicken on the grill and cook for 8 - 10 minutes or until done.

Serves: 4

Preparation time: 20 minutes

Indoor Grilling by Meriel Bradley :: www.MerielBradley.com

Chicken Kiev

4 chicken breasts
4 tablespoons butter
2 cloves garlic
3 tablespoons cornstarch
2 eggs beaten
2 cups breadcrumbs mixed
    with 4 tablespoons oil
2 tablespoons chopped fresh
    parsley
1 teaspoon salt

1 Crush garlic and salt into a paste.

2 Mix paste with butter and parsley.

3 Slit chicken breasts lengthwise to form a pocket.

4 Divide butter between each breast and place in the pocket.

5 Pre-heat grill.

6 Dip each breast into cornstarch, then egg, and then roll in breadcrumbs.

7 Place chicken on the grill and cook for 8 - 10 minutes or until done.

Serves: 4

Preparation time: 20 minutes

Beef

Ginger Beef

1 pound grilling steak cut
    into thin strips
2 tablespoons soy sauce
3 tablespoon dry wine
1 tablespoon brown sugar
1 inch ginger peeled and
    grated finely

1   Mix marinade ingredients together and add beef, coating well.

2   Allow to marinate for $\frac{1}{2}$ an hour.

3   Pre-heat grill.

4   Place beef on the grill and cook for 5 - 6 minutes or until done.

Serves: 4 \◯¶

Preparation time: 5 minutes ↻

Indoor Grilling by Meriel Bradley :: www.MerielBradley.com

Spicy Marinated Steak

4 small grilling steaks
1/3 cup red wine
2 tablespoons Worcestershire
  sauce
1/4 teaspoon ground black
  pepper
1/4 teaspoon Tabasco sauce
  (more if you like it hot!)
1/4 teaspoon salt

1 Mix marinade ingredients together and add beef, coating well.

2 Allow to marinate for 1/2 an hour.

3 Pre-heat grill.

4 Place beef on the grill and cook for 5 - 6 minutes or until done.

Serves: 4

Preparation time: 5 minutes

French Mustard Steaks

4 small grilling steaks
2 tablespoons whole grain
   Dijon mustard
2 tablespoons olive oil
4 tablespoons port or sweet
   red wine
Fresh ground salt to taste

1 Mix marinade ingredients together and add beef, coating well.

2 Allow to marinate in the refrigerator for $1/2$ an hour.

3 Pre-heat grill.

4 Place beef on the grill and cook for 5 - 6 minutes or until done.

Serves: 4

Preparation time: 5 minutes

Indoor Grilling by Meriel Bradley :: www.MerielBradley.com

Orange Garlic Beef

1 pound grilling steak cut
   into thin strips
²/₃ cup orange juice
2 cloves garlic mixed to a
   paste with 1 teaspoon salt
2 green scallions chopped
1 tablespoon olive oil

1 Mix orange juice with garlic and salt paste.

2 Add beef and scallions, coating well.

3 Allow to marinate in the refrigerator for ¹/₂ an hour.

4 Pre-heat grill.

5 Place beef on the grill and cook for 3 - 4 minutes or
until done.

QUICK TIP

*When slicing meat into
strips, cut thin slices across
the grain of the meat to
maintain tenderness.*

Serves: 4

Preparation time: 5 minutes

Beef Stir Fry

1 pound grilling steak
   sliced thin
1 clove garlic chopped
$1/2$ cup baby corn
$1/2$ cup water chestnuts sliced
$1/2$ red pepper sliced
$1/2$ green pepper sliced
$1/2$ cup chopped green
   scallions
$1/4$ cup red wine
3 tablespoons soy sauce
1 tablespoon brown sugar

1 Mix all ingredients together.

2 Allow to marinate for $1/2$ an hour.

3 Pre-heat grill.

4 Place the mixture on the grill and cook for 5 - 6 minutes or until done.

Serves: 4

Preparation time: 10 minutes

Indoor Grilling by Meriel Bradley :: www.MerielBradley.com

Tacos

½ pound lean ground beef
1 tablespoon rich soy sauce
1 onion, chopped
½ teaspoon ground black
    pepper
2 cloves garlic chopped

Sauce:
1 x 14 oz canned tomatoes
2 tsp vinegar
1 tablespoon tomato puree
1 tsp brown sugar
2 tsp paprika
1 small whole chili pepper
Taco shells
Optional: (heat to taste) use
    tabasco instead of whole
    chili pepper

1 Mix all sauce ingredients in a pan and simmer gently for
   30 minutes.

2 Pre-heat grill.

3 Combine ground beef, onion & garlic, soy sauce and
   black pepper.

4 Place ground beef on the grill and cook for 10 minutes or
   until done.

5 While beef is cooking, crisp taco shells in the oven.

6 Share ground beef and tomato mixes between tacos,
   putting ground beef in first.

7 Serve with diced tomato, cucumber and shredded lettuce.

Serves: 2

Preparation time: 15 minutes

Beef Fajitas

1 pound tender beef cut into strips
6 tablespoons lime juice
3 cloves crushed garlic
1-2 chili peppers or $1/4$ teaspoon chili powder
2 teaspoons ground cumin
2 tablespoons fresh chopped cilantro
3 tablespoons cooking oil
1 red onion thinly sliced
1 red pepper thinly sliced
1 green Pepper thinly sliced
1 yellow Pepper thinly sliced
4 - 8 tortillas

1 Mix beef strips, lime juice, garlic, chili peppers, cumin, cilantro and cooking oil together.

2 Marinade meat for at least 1 hour in the refrigerator (overnight is better).

3 Place onions and peppers on the top half of the grill, and beef strips on the bottom half. Cook for 4 - 5 minutes or until done.

4 Remove beef, peppers and onions from the grill and keep warm.

5 Place tortillas on the grill and heat for 1 minute.

6 Place tortillas on a plate. Add beef, onions and peppers.

7 Serve with salsa, sour cream, grated cheese and guacamole. Roll up and enjoy.

Serves: 4

Preparation time: 15 minutes

Indoor Grilling by Meriel Bradley :: *www.MerielBradley.com*

Stuffed Steak

4 small grilling steaks
1 large onion
1 1/2 cups breadcrumbs
4 sun-dried tomatoes,
  chopped (bottled in oil)
2 teaspoons dried Italian
  herb seasoning
1/2 teaspoon salt

1 Peel and slice onion, then place in a small pot, season and cover with water. Cook the onion until it begins to soften.

2 Lift the onion out and add to the other stuffing ingredients. Reserve the water.

3 Mix the stuffing ingredients adding the onion water as necessary to bind. Do not make the mixture too wet. Allow to cool before stuffing steak if not cooking steak right away.

4 Slit the steaks lengthwise to form a pocket.

5 Divide the stuffing between each steak and place in the pocket. Season steak with salt and pepper to taste.

6 Pre heat grill.

7 Place beef on the grill and cook for 7 - 8 minutes or until done.

Serves: 4

Preparation time: 20 minutes

Steak with Asparagus, Onions & Mushrooms

I Steak
6 asparagus spears, ends
    removed
6 mushrooms sliced
2 slices Spanish onion
I tablespoon Worcestershire
    sauce
Fresh ground pepper

1 Brush steak with Worcestershire sauce.

2 Press in the fresh ground pepper to taste.

3 Heat grill and place on the steak.

4 Place onions on top of the steak.

5 Place asparagus and mushrooms on the grill and cook until done.

Serves: 1

Preparation time: 10 minutes

Indoor Grilling by Meriel Bradley :: www.MerielBradley.com

Bacon London Broils

1 pound ground beef
1 medium onion very finely
   diced
2 tablespoons soft
   breadcrumbs
1 egg
$1/4$ teaspoon dried summer
   savory
1 teaspoon dried Italian
   seasoning
Salt and pepper to taste
4 slices bacon

1   Mix all ingredients except bacon together and form into 4 hamburger patties.

2   Wrap bacon around the outside of each patty and secure with a wooden cocktail stick.

3   Place on the grill.

4   Cook for 8 - 10 minutes or until done.

Serves: 4

Preparation time: 15 minutes

Steak in Red Wine Marinade

2 portions of your favorite
  grilling steak
$1/4$ cup soy sauce
$1/4$ cup red wine
$1/2$ teaspoon paprika
1 clove minced garlic
$1/4$ teaspoon summer savory

1 Mix marinade ingredients together and add beef, coating well.

2 Allow to marinate for at least 2 hours.

3 Pre-heat grill.

4 Place beef on the grill and cook for 5 - 6 minutes or until done.

QUICK TIP

When marinating be sure to turn foods a number of times to ensure all sides are equally exposed to the marinade.

Serves: 2

Preparation time: 5 minutes

Steak & Brandy

1 pound grilling steak
  sliced thin
2 green shallots chopped
$1/4$ cup brandy
1 tablespoon oil
1 tablespoon chopped fresh
  parsley
1 teaspoon Worcestershire
  sauce
Fresh ground salt and pepper
  to taste

1 Mix marinade ingredients together, then add beef and shallots, coating well.

2 Allow to marinate for $1/2$ an hour.

3 Pre-heat grill.

4 Place beef on the grill and cook for 4 - 5 minutes or until done.

Serves: 4

Preparation time: 5 minutes

Hamburgers

1 pound ground beef
2 tablespoons Worcestershire
sauce
1 onion chopped
1 egg beaten
1 teaspoon dried Italian herb
seasoning
Fresh ground salt and pepper
to taste

1 Mix all ingredients together.

2 Pre-heat grill.

3 Form mix into 4 large patties.

4 Place patties on the grill and cook for 5 - 6 minutes or
until done.

Serves: 4

Preparation time: 10 minutes

Indoor Grilling by Meriel Bradley :: www.MerielBradley.com

Steak & Pearl Onion Kebabs

1 pound grilling steak cubed
32 pearl onions peeled
$1/2$ cup tomato juice
1 clove garlic crushed with
    $1/2$ teaspoon salt
1 tablespoon soy sauce
1 teaspoon mustard
1 tablespoon tomato puree
$1/4$ teaspoon oregano
Fresh ground pepper to taste

1 Soak 8 bamboo skewers in water for $1/2$ an hour.

2 Thread skewers with beef and onions.

3 Mix seasonings and pour over skewers.

4 Leave to marinate for $1/2$ an hour.

5 Pre-heat grill.

6 Place skewers on the grill and cook for 5 - 6 minutes or until done.

Serves: 2 - 4

Preparation time: 15 minutes

Mixed Grill Kebab

1/4 pound grilling steak cubed
2 large pork sausages cut
    into 4 pieces each
2 small onions peeled and
    cut into 4
16 small mushrooms
16 cherry tomatoes
1/2 cup wine
4 tablespoons olive oil
1/2 tablespoon dried oregano
Fresh ground salt and pepper
    to taste

1 Soak 8 bamboo skewers in water for 1/2 an hour.

2 Thread skewers with beef, sausages, onions, mushrooms and tomatoes.

3 Mix seasonings and pour over skewers.

4 Allow to marinate for 1/2 an hour.

5 Pre-heat grill.

6 Place skewers on the grill and cook for 5 - 6 minutes or until done.

QUICK TIP

If using wooden skewers on a grill, soak them in water for 20 - 30 minutes to prevent them from burning during cooking.

Serves: 2 - 4

Preparation time: 10 minutes

Indoor Grilling by Meriel Bradley :: www.MerielBradley.com

Pork

Pork Kebabs

1 pound pork cubed
Juice 1 lemon
4 tablespoons olive oil
1 teaspoon dried oregano
$^1/_4$ teaspoon salt

1 Soak 8 bamboo skewers in water for $^1/_2$ an hour.

2 Thread skewers with pork.

3 Mix seasonings and pour over skewers.

4 Allow to marinate for $^1/_2$ an hour.

5 Pre-heat grill.

6 Place skewers on the grill and cook for 5 - 6 minutes or until done.

Serves: 2 - 4

Preparation time: 10 minutes

Pork, Sausage & Pepper Kebabs

$^1/_2$ pound pork cubed

4 large sausages cut into 4 pieces each

1 green pepper cut into $1^1/_2$ inch squares

1 red pepper cut into $1^1/_2$ inch squares

4 tablespoons olive oil

$^1/_2$ cup white wine

$^1/_2$ tablespoon dried summer savory

$^1/_4$ teaspoon salt

1 Soak 8 bamboo skewers in water for $^1/_2$ an hour.

2 Thread skewers with pork, sausage and peppers.

3 Mix seasonings and pour over skewers.

4 Allow to marinate for $^1/_2$ an hour.

5 Pre-heat grill.

6 Place skewers on the grill and cook for 5 - 6 minutes or until done.

Serves: 2 - 4

Preparation time: 10 minutes

Honey Pineapple Ham Steaks

4 small ham steaks
$^1/_2$ cup pineapple juice
4 tablespoons honey
4 cloves
8 rings pineapple

1 Mix pineapple juice, honey and cloves together.

2 Add ham steaks and marinate for $^1/_2$ an hour.

3 Pre-heat grill.

4 Place ham steaks on the grill, adding 2 rings of pineapple to each.

5 Cook for 5 - 6 minutes or until done.

Serves: 4

Preparation time: 10 minutes

Apricot Glazed Ham Steaks

4 small ham steaks
16 apricots soaked in the
    apple juice and brandy
    over night
1 cup apple juice
$\frac{1}{2}$ cup brandy
8 cloves
2 tablespoons brown sugar
2 tablespoons mustard mixed
    with 2 tablespoons
    apple juice and
    2 tablespoons wine

1 Place the apricot mix in a small pot and add the cloves and sugar. Top up with apple juice if necessary to cover the apricots.

2 Bring to a boil, and then turn down to a simmer until apricots start to soften.

3 Remove from heat and cover.

4 Pre heat grill.

5 Coat ham steaks with mustard mix and grill for 4 - 5 minutes or until done.

6 Transfer to a serving dish and pour apricot mixture over ham steaks.

Serves: 4

Preparation time: 20 minutes

Lemon Dill Pork Chops

4 butterfly pork chops
$1/2$ cup lemon juice
2 scallions chopped
1 tablespoon fresh dill
    chopped
1 tablespoon fresh cilantro
    chopped
Fresh ground salt to taste

1 Mix marinade ingredients together, then add pork, coating well.

2 Allow to marinate for $1/2$ an hour.

3 Pre-heat grill.

4 Place pork on the grill and cook for 5 - 6 minutes or until done.

Serves: 4

Preparation time: 5 minutes

Indoor Grilling by Meriel Bradley :: www.MerielBradley.com

Spicy Pork Chops

4 butterfly pork chops
4 tablespoons natural yogurt
1 teaspoon red curry paste
   (more if you like it hotter)
Juice ½ lime
¼ teaspoon salt

1 Mix marinade ingredients together and add pork, coating well.

2 Allow to marinate for ½ an hour.

3 Pre-heat grill.

4 Place pork on the grill and cook for 5 - 6 minutes or until done.

Serves: 4

Preparation time: 5 minutes

Port & Berry Chops

4 butterfly pork chops
1 cup port
1 tablespoon blackcurrant jam
1/4 teaspoon salt

1. Mix marinade ingredients together and add pork, coating well.

2. Allow to marinate for 1/2 an hour.

3. Pre-heat grill.

4. Place pork on the grill and cook for 5 - 6 minutes or until done.

QUICK TIP

Cooking times are approximate only – adjust times to suit your grill.

Serves: 4

Preparation time: 5 minutes

Sausage & Lemon Stuffing Burgers

1 cup soft breadcrumbs
1 pound sausage meat
Zest of 2 lemons (grate the
    rind if you don't have a
    zester)
1 teaspoon dried oregano
1 teaspoon dried thyme

1 Mix all ingredients together.

2 Pre-heat grill.

3 Form into small patties and place on the grill and cook for
6 - 7 minutes or until done.

Serves: 4

Preparation time: 10 minutes

Pork Ribs

Pork ribs to serve 2
3/4 cup tomato juice
1/3 cup water
1 tablespoon oil
1 teaspoon garlic powder
2 tablespoons soy sauce
2 tablespoons red wine
1 teaspoon sugar
2 tablespoons tomato paste
1/4 teaspoon Tabasco sauce
Fresh ground pepper to taste

QUICK TIP
Always discard any remaining marinade. Never re-use.

1 Mix all ingredients together and pour over pork ribs.

2 Allow to marinate for a minimum of 2 hours before grilling.

3 Place ribs on the grill and cook for 20 - 30 minutes or until done.

Makes: 1 1/2 cups

Preparation time: 10 minutes

Indoor Grilling by Meriel Bradley :: www.MerielBradley.com

Cumin-Yogurt Pork Chops

2 pork chops
2 tablespoons natural yogurt
1 clove garlic crushed
$1/4$ teaspoon cumin
$1/4$ teaspoon salt
Zest of $1/2$ lime

1 Mix all marinade ingredients together.

2 Add pork chops and allow to marinade for a minimum of 2 hours.

3 Pre-heat grill.

4 Place pork chops on the grill and cook for 6 - 8 minutes or until done.

Serves: 2

Preparation time: 10 minutes

Pork Stuffed with Sage & Onion

4 center-cut boneless
   butterfly pork chops
1 large onion peeled and
   cut into quarters
1½ cups breadcrumbs
2 tablespoons chopped
   fresh sage
8 slices bacon
Fresh ground salt and pepper
   to taste

1 In a small pot cover onion with water, add a little salt, and cook until the onion just starts to soften.

2 Mix breadcrumbs, sage, and seasonings in a bowl.

3 Lift onion out of the water and add to the other ingredients, then bind with the onion water as needed. Do not let it become too wet. Allow to cool before stuffing pork if not cooking right away.

4 Pre-heat grill.

5 Place ¼ of the stuffing mix on one half of each pork chop. Fold the other half over, and wrap 2 pieces of bacon around each one.

6 Place on the grill and cook for 10 - 12 minutes or until done.

Serves: 4

Preparation time: 20 minutes

Pork Stuffed with Onion & Apple

4 boneless centre cut
  butterfly pork chops
1 large onion peeled and cut
  into quarters
2 dessert apples peeled
  and diced
2 teaspoons sugar
1 teaspoon fresh chopped sage
8 slices bacon
Fresh ground salt and pepper
  to taste

1 In a small pot cover onion with water, add a little salt, and cook until the onion just starts to soften.

2 Lift onion out of the water and mix with apples, sugar, sage and seasonings. Allow to cool before stuffing pork if not cooking right away.

3 Pre-heat grill.

4 Place $1/4$ of the stuffing mix on one half of each pork chop. Fold the other half over, and wrap 2 pieces of bacon around each one.

5 Place on the grill and cook for 10 - 12 minutes or until done.

QUICK TIP
Recipes in this book are designed for electric contact grills. If cooking on an open grid barbecue or gas grill, use foil where necessary and adjust cooking times accordingly.

Serves: 4

Preparation time: 20 minutes

Pork Stuffed with Tomato & Rice

4 boneless centre cut
   butterfly pork chops
1 cup cooked rice
1 small onion diced
1 tomato diced
½ red pepper diced
1 tablespoon butter
1 teaspoon dried Italian herb
   seasoning
8 slices bacon
Fresh ground salt and pepper
   to taste

1. In a small pot melt butter, then add onion and peppers. Cook for 2 - 3 minutes.

2. In a bowl mix the rice, tomato and seasonings. Allow to cool before stuffing pork if not cooking right away.

3. Add onions and peppers.

4. Pre-heat grill.

5. Place ¼ of the stuffing mix on one half of each pork chop. Fold the other half over, and wrap 2 pieces of bacon around each one.

6. Place on the grill and cook for 10 - 12 minutes or until done.

Serves: 4

Preparation time: 20 minutes

Indoor Grilling by Meriel Bradley :: www.MerielBradley.com

Vegetables

Spicy Potato Wedges

1½ pounds yellow flesh
   potatoes washed and
   sliced into wedges
⅓ cup olive oil
1 teaspoon dried parsley
¼ teaspoon salt
½ teaspoon fresh ground
   black pepper
½ teaspoon chili powder
   (more or less to taste)

1 Pre-heat grill.

2 Mix the potato wedges and seasonings together.

3 Place potato wedges on the grill and cook for 15 - 18 minutes or until done.

Serves: 2 - 4

Preparation time: 10 minutes

Indoor Grilling by Meriel Bradley :: www.MerielBradley.com

Mixed Vegetables with Ginger

1 zucchini sliced into strips
1 cup broccoli cut into small
    florets
1 cup cauliflower cut into
    small florets
1 cup sugar snap peas
2 tablespoons olive oil
2 tablespoon soy sauce
1 teaspoon finely grated
    ginger root

1 Pre-heat grill.

2 Mix vegetables and seasonings together.

3 Place vegetables on the grill and cook for 10 - 12 minutes or until desired softness is reached.

Serves: 2 - 4

Preparation time: 10 minutes

Lemon Garlic Asparagus

1 pound asparagus
Juice $\frac{1}{2}$ lemon
2 tablespoons melted butter
$\frac{1}{2}$ teaspoon garlic salt

1 Pre-heat grill.

2 Mix lemon juice, butter and garlic salt together.

3 Toss asparagus in the mixture (the butter will set on the asparagus as you toss it).

4 Place coated asparagus on the grill and cook for 5 - 6 minutes, or until desired softness is reached.

QUICK TIP

When grilling, check you food to see if it is done SOONER rather than later. You can always put food back on the grill if it is not cooked through, but you cannot reconstitute overcooked foods.

Serves: 4

Preparation time: 5 minutes

Indoor Grilling by Meriel Bradley :: www.MerielBradley.com

Herby Eggplant

1 large eggplant cut into strips
1 clove garlic crushed
1 tablespoon fresh chopped
    parsley
$1/2$ tablespoon fresh basil
$1/2$ tablespoon fresh thyme
2 tablespoons olive oil
Fresh ground salt and pepper
    to taste

1 Pre-heat grill.

2 Mix all ingredients in a bowl, coating eggplant well.

3 Place eggplant on the grill and cook for 5 - 6 minutes, or until desired softness is reached.

Serves: 2 - 4

Preparation time: 10 minutes

Vegetable Kebabs

16 pearl onions peeled
16 small mushrooms
16 cherry tomatoes
1 red pepper cut into 8 pieces
1 green pepper cut into
    8 pieces
2 zucchini cut into 8 pieces
    each
3/4 cup white wine
4 tablespoons olive oil
1 tablespoon fresh chopped
    chives
1 tablespoon fresh chopped
    cilantro
Fresh ground salt and pepper
    to taste

1 Soak 8 bamboo skewers in water for 1/2 an hour.

2 Thread skewers with the vegetables.

3 Mix seasonings, and pour over the skewers.

4 Allow to marinate for 1/2 an hour.

5 Pre-heat grill.

6 Place skewers on the grill and cook for 5 - 6 minutes or until done.

Serves: 4

Preparation time: 15 minutes

Indoor Grilling by Meriel Bradley :: www.MerielBradley.com

Stuffed Mushrooms

10 large white mushrooms
    with the stalks removed
1/2 cup crumbled feta cheese
3 tablespoons bacon bits or
    crumbled bacon
1 teaspoon dried Italian herb
    seasoning

1 Pre-heat grill.

2 Cut a thin slice from the rounded top of each mushroom to stop it rocking on the grill.

3 Mix cheese, bacon and herbs together.

4 Fill mushrooms and place on grill.

5 Cook for 4 - 5 minutes or until the mushrooms start to soften.

Serves: 2 - 4

Preparation time: 5 minutes

Mediterranean Grilled Vegetables

1 small eggplant cut into
    strips
$^1/_2$ green pepper sliced
$^1/_2$ red pepper sliced
$^1/_2$ yellow pepper sliced
$^1/_4$ red Spanish onion sliced
3 tablespoons olive oil
1 tablespoon lemon juice
$^1/_2$ tablespoon oregano
Fresh ground salt and pepper
    to taste

1 Pre-heat grill.

2 Toss the vegetables in the oil, lemon juice, oregano and fresh ground salt and pepper.

3 Place vegetables on the grill and cook for 5 - 6 minutes or until desired tenderness is reached.

Serves: 4

Preparation time: 10 minutes

Indoor Grilling by Meriel Bradley :: www.MerielBradley.com

Pea & Bean Stir Fry

1 cup snow peas
1 cup sliced green beans
1 clove garlic crushed to a
   paste with 2 teaspoons salt
1 teaspoon sugar
1 tablespoon olive oil

1 Pre-heat grill.

2 Toss all ingredients together.

3 Place vegetables on the grill and cook for 3 - 4 minutes or until vegetables reach desired tenderness.

Serves: 2 - 4

Preparation time: 10 minutes

Barbecue Onions

2 large Spanish onions peeled
   and sliced into rings
   (approx. 8 slices, do not
   separate into rings)
3 tablespoons barbecue sauce
2 tablespoons melted butter

1. Pre-heat grill.

2. Mix barbecue sauce and butter together.

3. Brush over onions and place on grill.

4. Cook for 8 - 10 minutes, or until desired softness is reached (you may wish to brush more of the sauce over the onions while cooking).

5. Serve with steak, hamburgers or hotdogs.

Serves: 4 - 6

Preparation time: 5 minutes

Red Potatoes

1 pound red potatoes
washed and sliced
$^1/_3$ cup olive oil
3 tablespoons dried parsley
1 teaspoon paprika
$^1/_2$ teaspoon celery salt
$^1/_4$ teaspoon fresh ground
pepper

1 Pre-heat grill.

2 In a large bowl toss potatoes in seasonings.

3 Place potatoes on the grill and cook for 15 - 20 minutes or until soft.

QUICK TIP

Measure spices over the sink to prevent spilling excess into your meal preparation.

Serves: 2 - 4

Preparation time: 10 minutes

Potatoes and Mushrooms with Fresh Herbs

6 Yukon gold or yellow flesh
  potato sliced into 'chips'
1 pound white mushrooms
  sliced
2 tablespoons butter
1 tablespoon olive oil
1 tablespoon fresh chopped
  basil
1 tablespoon fresh chopped
  thyme
2 tablespoons fresh chopped
  parsley

1 Pre-heat grill.

2 In a sauce pan, melt butter, then add olive oil, basil, thyme and parsley.

3 Mix potatoes and mushrooms together, then pour the butter mixture over and stir.

4 Place potatoes and mushrooms on the grill and cook for 10 - 12 minutes or until potatoes are soft.

QUICK TIP

To freeze fresh herbs wash them, chop them up, and pat them dry. Then spread them out on a double layer of paper towel on a cookie sheet and place them in the freezer. Once frozen, place in a freezer bag and return to freezer.

Serves: 3

Preparation time: 10 minutes

Indoor Grilling by Meriel Bradley :: www.MerielBradley.com

Sweet Potatoes & Apple

2 large sweet potatoes
6 granny smith apples
$^1/_3$ cup brown sugar
2 tablespoons olive oil
$^1/_3$ cup brandy (optional)

1. Peel sweet potatoes and slice into $^1/_2$ inch thick rings.

2. Peel and core apples and slice into $^1/_2$ inch thick rings.

3. Place apple and sweet potato slices in a dish. Sprinkle on brown sugar and pour brandy over.

4. Pre-heat grill.

5. Place sweet potatoes on grill and cook for 5 - 6 minutes or until just starting to soften.

6. Add apples and cook for another 2 - 3 minutes or until apples and sweet potatoes are soft.

Serves: 3 - 4

Preparation time: 15 minutes

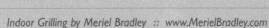

Mashed Potato Cakes

1 onion finely diced
2 pounds potatoes peeled
   (Yukon Gold or yellow
   flesh potatoes have great
   flavor)
2 tablespoons butter
Milk for mixing
Fresh ground salt and pepper
   to taste

1 Cut potatoes into pieces and steam or boil until soft.

2 Add butter and seasonings and mash with a potato masher.

3 Add enough milk to obtain a creamy consistency, and continue mashing until no lumps remain. Add onion and allow to cool.

4 Form into cakes and place in refrigerator for 1 - 2 hours.

5 Brush grill with oil and pre-heat.

6 Place potato cakes on the grill and cook for 5 - 6 minutes.

Serves: 4 - 6

Preparation time: 15 minutes

Grated
Potato Cakes

1 medium onion thinly sliced
3½ cups peeled and grated
    potatoes
1½ cups shredded cheese
1 tablespoon olive oil
Fresh ground pepper to taste

1 Place grated potatoes on a double thickness of paper towels to remove excess moisture. They must be dry.

2 Mix all ingredients together.

3 Pre-heat grill.

4 Divide into 8 - 4 inch patties and place on grill.

5 Cook until golden brown on each side and potato is cooked through.

Serves: 4 - 6

Preparation time: 15 minutes

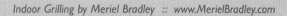

Bacon-Wrapped Vegetables

4 scallions
2 zucchini cut lengthwise
    intro strips
12 asparagus spears
4 slices bacon

1   Divide vegetables into 4 bundles.

2   Pre-heat grill.

3   Wrap 1 piece of bacon around each bundle and secure with a wooden cocktail stick.

4   Place bundles on the grill and cook for 5 - 6 minutes or until bacon is done.

Serves: 2 - 4

Preparation time: 10 minutes

Indoor Grilling by Meriel Bradley :: www.MerielBradley.com

Desserts

Fruit Kebabs

32 strawberries
32 pineapple chunks
32 banana chunks
32 apricot halves
1 cup sweet port
Melted chocolate to garnish

1. Soak 8 bamboo skewers in water for $1/2$ an hour.

2. Thread skewers with fruit.

3. Pour port over skewers.

4. Leave to marinate for $1/2$ an hour.

5. Pre-heat grill.

6. Place on skewers and cook for 5 - 6 minutes, leaving grill open.

7. Brush remaining port over fruit while cooking, turning skewers as you go.

8. Drizzle with melted chocolate and serve with whipped cream.

Serves: 2 - 4

Preparation time: 10 minutes

Indoor Grilling by Meriel Bradley :: www.MerielBradley.com

Chocolate Bananas

4 bananas in their skins
1 large bar chocolate
  (your favorite)
4 tablespoons brandy

1 Pre-heat grill.

2 Lay the banana on its side. Leaving the skin on, make a slit along the length of each banana.

3 Break chocolate into squares and place in slits along the length of the banana.

4 Pour 1 tablespoon of brandy into each banana.

5 Place bananas on the grill and cook for 5 - 6 minutes or until chocolate has melted.

6 Serve bananas in the skin. Eat with a spoon.

Serves: 4

Preparation time: 5 minutes

Rum & Raisin Bananas

4 bananas in their skins
8 tablespoons raisins
4 tablespoons rum
4 tablespoons brown sugar

1 Pre-heat grill.

2 Lay the banana on its side. Leaving the skin on, make a slit along the length of each banana.

3 Place 2 tablespoons of raisins in slits along the length of each banana.

4 Pour 1 tablespoon of rum into each banana.

5 Sprinkle 1 tablespoon of sugar into each banana.

6 Place bananas on the grill and cook for 5 - 6 minutes or until sugar has melted.

7 Serve bananas in the skin. Eat with a spoon.

Serves: 4

Preparation time: 5 minutes

Indoor Grilling by Meriel Bradley :: www.MerielBradley.com

Griddle Scones

2 cups flour
4 teaspoons baking powder
1/4 teaspoon salt
4 tablespoons butter
2 tablespoons sugar
1/2 cup raisins
Milk to mix

1 Mix flour, baking powder, salt and sugar together.

2 Cut butter into flour mix until it resembles fine crumbs.

3 Stir in raisins.

4 Mix to a soft rolling consistency with milk.

5 Pre-heat grill.

6 Roll dough to 1/3 inch thick on a floured board.

7 Cut into desired shapes.

8 Place on grill but do not close lid.

9 Cook for 9 minutes per side or until done. Scones should sound hollow when tapped.

Serves: 4 - 6

Preparation time: 15 minutes

QUICK TIP

Make a meal plan for the week and plan your shopping lists so you will always have the ingredients you need, and eliminate any wasted food.

Apple Fritters

1 cup flour
4 tablespoons sugar
2 teaspoons baking powder
$^1/_4$ teaspoon salt
$^2/_3$ cup milk
1 egg
2 tablespoons butter
3 large cooking apples
2 tablespoons of flour mixed
  with 1 tablespoon of sugar
  and 1 tablespoon cinnamon
Lime juice and sugar to serve

1 In a large bowl, sift the first 3 ingredients together.

2 Beat egg and milk together, add to the bowl and beat until smooth.

3 Melt butter and mix in.

4 Pre-heat grill.

5 Peel and core apples and slice into rings.

6 Dust with flour, sugar & cinnamon mix.

7 Lightly spray grill with oil.

8 Dip each ring into the batter and place on grill. Cook for 4 - 5 minutes or until golden.

9 Sprinkle with lime juice, sugar, and serve.

Serves: 4 - 6

Preparation time: 15 minutes

Indoor Grilling by Meriel Bradley :: www.MerielBradley.com

Nutty Caramel Apricots

32 apricot halves, fresh or
   canned (stone removed)
4 tablespoons butter
4 tablespoons brown sugar
4 tablespoons chopped
   pecans
1 teaspoon cinnamon

1 Pre-heat grill.

2 In a bowl, whisk butter, sugar and cinnamon together.
Add nuts and mix in.

3 Stuff each apricot half with the butter mix and place second
half on top.

4 Place apricots on the grill and cook for 2 minutes or until
sugar has melted.

5 Serve with low fat yogurt or whipped cream.

Serves: 2 - 4

Preparation time: 5 minutes

Caramel Bananas

4 bananas cut in $\frac{1}{2}$ then in $\frac{1}{2}$ lengthwise
4 tablespoons melted butter
4 teaspoons soft brown sugar
$\frac{1}{3}$ cup melted chocolate or store bought chocolate topping

1 Preheat grill.

2 Place melted butter and bananas in a bowl.

3 Gently turn bananas to coat with butter.

4 While continuing to gently turn bananas, sprinkle on sugar to coat.

5 Place bananas carefully on grill, taking care not to break them. Cook until sugar has caramelized (it will look like soft toffee).

6 Remove from grill, drizzle with melted chocolate and serve with low fat yogurt or whipped cream.

Serves: 4

Preparation time: 10 minutes

Stuffed Grilled Apples

4 dessert apples
8 tablespoons pecans
   chopped
4 tablespoons honey
4 tablespoons brown sugar
2 tablespoons butter
1 teaspoon cinnamon

1 Pre-heat grill.

2 Cut each apple in ½ and remove core.

3 In a small bowl, blend remaining ingredients to a paste.

4 Divide the mixture between the apples and fill the centers.

5 Place apples on the grill and cook for 5 - 6 minutes or until the sugar has melted.

Serves: 4

Preparation time: 10 minutes

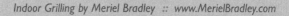

Waffles
with Fruit

4 waffles
1 cup sliced strawberries
1 cup blueberries
1 cup maple syrup or
   chocolate sauce – both if
   you are feeling decadent
½ cup whipped cream

1 Pre-heat grill.

2 Place waffles on the grill and cook for 3 - 4 minutes or until nicely browned.

3 Divide fruit between the waffles and pile on.

4 Add cream and pour on syrup or sauce.

Serves: 4

Preparation time: 10 minutes

Indoor Grilling by Meriel Bradley :: www.MerielBradley.com

Maple Nut Waffles

4 waffles
1 cup toasted walnuts
8 scoops ice cream
1 cup maple syrup or
    chocolate sauce – both if
    you are feeling decadent

1 Pre-heat grill.

2 Place waffles on the grill and cook for 3 - 4 minutes or
until nicely browned.

3 Place 2 scoops of ice cream on each waffle.

4 Add walnuts and pour on syrup or sauce.

QUICK TIP

*Plan ahead and make a
double or triple recipe, and
freeze in portions ready for
those hectic days.*

Serves: 4

Preparation time: 10 minutes

Grilled Pineapple

1 pound pineapple spears
  (tinned or fresh)
¹/₂ cup rum
¹/₂ cup honey
4 tablespoons brown sugar

1 Pre-heat grill.

2 In a bowl, whisk rum, honey and sugar together.

3 Add pineapple and allow to soak for ¹/₂ an hour.

4 Place pineapple on the grill.

5 Cook for 2 - 3 minutes or until bubbly.

Serves: 4 - 6

Preparation time: 5 minutes

Snacks

French Toast

1 egg
¹/₂ cup milk
¹/₂ teaspoon vanilla
¹/₄ teaspoon cinnamon
4 slices bread

1 Beat egg, then mix in other ingredients.

2 Pre-heat grill.

3 Dip bread in mixture, covering each side, then place on grill.

4 Cook until lightly browned.

5 Serve with fresh fruit and maple syrup.

Serves: 2 - 4

Preparation time: 5 minutes

Indoor Grilling by Meriel Bradley :: www.MerielBradley.com

Banana Toast

1 egg
1/2 cup milk
1/2 teaspoon vanilla
1/2 teaspoon cinnamon
1 small banana mashed
4 slices bread

1 Beat egg, then mix in other ingredients.

2 Pre-heat grill.

3 Dip bread in mixture, covering each side, then place on grill.

4 Cook until lightly browned.

5 Serve with fresh fruit and maple syrup.

Serves: 2 - 4

Preparation time: 5 minutes

Sandwiches

The Perfect BLT

4-6 strips bacon
2 lettuce leaves washed
 and dried
2-4 slices tomato
2 slices fresh bread
Mayonnaise

1 Cook bacon on the grill until crisp.

2 Spread a little mayonnaise on each piece of bread.

3 Layer lettuce, tomato and bacon on the first piece of bread and sandwich with the second.

Serves: 4

Preparation time: 10 minutes

Indoor Grilling by Meriel Bradley :: www.MerielBradley.com

Grilled Vegetable Sandwiches

4 onion buns
4 slices provolone or swiss
    cheese
4 slices eggplant
$^1/_2$ green pepper sliced
$^1/_2$ red pepper sliced
$^1/_4$ red Spanish onion sliced
8 mushrooms sliced
1 tablespoon parmesan cheese
2 tablespoons olive oil
1 tablespoon white wine
Fresh ground salt and pepper
    to taste

QUICK TIP

*If you make a packed lunch,
cook extra meat and
vegetables at dinner time for
your sandwich the next day.*

1   Pre-heat the grill.

2   Toss the vegetables in the oil, wine and fresh ground salt and pepper.

3   Place on the grill and sprinkle on the parmesan cheese.

4   Cook for 5 - 6 minutes. Remove from grill.

5   Cut the onion buns in half and add a slice of cheese to each one.

6   Divide the vegetables between each bun and replace the top halves.

Serves: 4

Preparation time: 10 minutes

Pastrami & Swiss

8 slices rye bread
4 slices Swiss cheese
6 oz shaved pastrami
4 tablespoons sauerkraut
2 tablespoons mayonnaise
$1/2$ teaspoon Tabasco sauce
Butter for spreading

1 Butter one side of each piece of bread.

2 Place 4 pieces butter side down on a board.

3 Mix mayonnaise with Tabasco sauce and spread on 4 slices of bread.

4 Divide pastrami between 4 slices, then add sauerkraut.

5 Add Swiss cheese and the last 4 pieces of bread, butter side up.

6 Place sandwiches on the grill and cook for 4 - 5 minutes or until cheese has melted.

Serves: 4

Preparation time: 10 minutes

Indoor Grilling by Meriel Bradley :: www.MerielBradley.com

Feta Cheese & Roasted Red Peppers

2 Italian buns
1 small jar roasted red
   peppers chopped
$1/2$ cup crumbled feta cheese

1 Pre-heat grill.

2 Cut buns in $1/2$ and pull out some the bread from the inside.

3 Fill with roasted red peppers and feta cheese.

4 Place buns on the grill and cook for 2 - 3 minutes.

Serves: 2 - 4

Preparation time: 5 minutes

Smoked Salmon & Cheese

2 Italian buns
8 slices smoked salmon
¹/₂ cup crumbled feta

1 Pre-heat grill.

2 Cut Italian buns in ¹/₂ and pull out some the bread from the inside.

3 Fill with smoked salmon and feta cheese.

4 Place buns on the grill and cook for 2 - 3 minutes.

Serves: 4

Preparation time: 5 minutes

Indoor Grilling by Meriel Bradley :: www.MerielBradley.com

Chicken & Grilled Zucchini Wrap

¼ pound chicken strips
1 zucchini slice into strips
2 tablespoons soy sauce
1 teaspoon brown sugar
¼ teaspoon dried oregano
2 fajita wraps

1 Pre-heat grill.

2 Mix all ingredients except zucchini and fajita wraps together.

3 Place the mix on the grill and spread out, then place the zucchini at the top of the grill.

4 Cook for 4 - 5 minutes, or until the chicken is done.

5 Remove the chicken and zucchini from the grill.

6 Place wraps on the grill for 30 seconds to warm.

7 Divide the chicken and zucchini between the 2 wraps and roll up.

Serves: 2

Preparation time: 10 minutes

Crab Meat & Grilled Zucchini Wrap

1 can crab meat
2 zucchini cut into strips
$1/2$ cup finely shredded lettuce
1 tablespoon olive oil
$1/2$ tablespoon soy sauce
1 teaspoon dried chives
2 fajita wraps
Fresh ground salt and pepper
to taste

1. Pre-heat grill.

2. Pour oil and soy sauce over zucchini, then sprinkle on chives and fresh ground salt and pepper to taste.

3. Place zucchini on the grill and cook for 3 - 4 minutes or until just starting to soften. Then add the crab meat to heat through.

4. Remove zucchini and crab meat, and add wraps to the grill for 30 seconds to warm.

5. Divide zucchini, crab meat and lettuce between the 2 wraps and roll up.

Serves: 2

Preparation time: 10 minutes

Indoor Grilling by Meriel Bradley :: www.MerielBradley.com

Beef & Grilled Mushroom & Onion Wrap

$^1/_4$ pound grilling beef strips
$^1/_2$ small red onion sliced
$^1/_2$ pound mushrooms sliced
2 tablespoons Worcestershire
  sauce
1 teaspoon brown sugar
$^1/_4$ teaspoon dried oregano
2 fajita wraps

1 Pre-heat grill.

2 Mix all ingredients together.

3 Place the mix on the grill and spread out.

4 Cook for 4 - 5 minutes, or until the beef is no longer pink in the middle.

5 Remove the mix.

6 Place wraps on the grill for 30 seconds to warm.

7 Divide the mix between the 2 wraps and roll up.

QUICK TIP
Always use fresh foods when freezing – never refreeze foods.

Serves: 2

Preparation time: 10 minutes

Portobello Mushroom Sandwich

4 Portobello mushrooms
4 slices provolone cheese
1 small jar roasted red peppers
8 spinach leaves
2 tablespoons chopped fresh
    basil leaves
1/2 cup Caesar dressing
4 onion buns split

1. Pre-heat grill.

2. Wash mushrooms and remove stalks.

3. Pour Caesar dressing over mushrooms.

4. Place on the grill and cook for 3 - 4 minutes or until tender.

5. Place red peppers on the grill for the last 1 minute of cooking.

6. Place mushrooms on the bottom half of the bun and add a cheese slice to each.

7. Divide the red peppers, spinach and basil between the buns.

8. Place top half of the bun on top and serve.

Serves: 4

Preparation time: 5 minutes

Indoor Grilling by Meriel Bradley :: www.MerielBradley.com

Grilled Cheese & Tomato

8 slices bread
1 cup shredded cheese
1/2 cup diced tomatoes
Butter for the bread
(optional)

1 Pre-heat grill.

2 Butter 8 slices of bread.

3 Divide cheese and tomato between the first four slices and place on the un-buttered side.

4 Place the remaining four slices on top (butter-side up) to complete the sandwiches.

5 Place on the grill and cook for 2 - 3 minutes or until cheese has melted.

Serves: 2 - 4

Preparation time: 5 minutes

Grilled Cheese, Ham & Onion

8 slices rye bread
1 cup shredded cheese
1/2 cup chopped ham
1/4 cup finely chopped onion
Butter for the bread (optional)

1. Pre-heat grill.

2. Butter 8 slices of bread.

3. Divide cheese, ham and onion between the first four slices and place on the un-buttered side.

4. Place the remaining four slices on top (butter-side up) to complete the sandwiches.

5. Place on the grill and cook for 2 - 3 minutes or until cheese has melted.

Serves: 2 - 4

Preparation time: 5 minutes

Indoor Grilling by Meriel Bradley :: www.MerielBradley.com

Grilled Pizza Cheese

8 slices white bread
1 cup shredded cheese
$^1/_2$ cup chopped pepperoni
$^1/_4$ cup diced tomatoes
Butter for the bread (optional)

1 Pre-heat grill.

2 Butter 8 slices of bread.

3 Divide cheese, pepperoni and tomato between the first four slices and place on the un-buttered side.

4 Place the remaining four slices on top (butter-side up) to complete the sandwiches.

5 Place on the grill and cook for 2 - 3 minutes or until cheese has melted.

QUICK TIP

When making a meal plan for the week, use one or two recipes that can be doubled or tripled for freezing, so you can build up your freezer stock with homemade freezer meals.

Serves: 2 - 4

Preparation time: 5 minutes

More
Meriel Bradley!

Please turn this page
for a bonus excerpt from

DESSERTS

the next volume in
Meriel Bradley's popular
cookbook series

Desserts

Banana Raisin Loaf

8 tablespoons butter
1 cup sugar
2 eggs
2 cups flour
2 teaspoons baking powder
$1/2$ teaspoon salt
1 teaspoon vanilla
2 large bananas mashed
1 cup raisins
Milk or buttermilk to mix

1. Pre-heat the oven to 350 degrees F.

2. Cream butter and sugar together until light and fluffy.

3. Add the eggs one at a time beating well after each addition.

4. Add the bananas and vanilla, mix in well.

5. Sift the dry ingredients together and fold into the banana mixture.

6. Add the raisins and fold in.

7. Add enough milk to form a mixture that will drop easily from a spoon.

8. Pour into a greased loaf pan and bake for 50 – 60 minutes or until a wooden pick inserted in the centre comes out clean.

Makes: 1 loaf

Preparation time: 20 minutes

Strawberry Peach Crumble

Filling
1 1/2 cups strawberries halved
1 can peaches in juice
   (approx 14 oz)
2 tablespoons honey
1/8 teaspoon cinnamon

Topping
1/2 cup brown sugar
1/2 cup butter
1/2 cup coconut
1 1/4 cups flour

1. Drain the peaches and mix 1/2 cup of the juice with the honey and cinnamon.

2. Place the peaches and strawberries in a 9 inch pie dish and pour over the honey, cinnamon and juice mixture.

3. Pre-heat the oven to 325 degrees F.

4. In a bowl cream the sugar and butter together.

5. Add the flour a little at a time to make a crumbly mixture.

6. Mix in the coconut.

7. Sprinkle the mixture over the fruit in the pie dish.

8. Place in the oven and cook for 35 – 45 minutes until the fruit is bubbling and the top is golden.

9. Place foil over the top if it starts to over brown.

Serves: 4 - 6

Preparation time: 15 minutes

Desserts by Meriel Bradley :: www.MerielBradley.com

Nutty Shortbread

1¼ cup soft butter
1¼ cups brown sugar
2 cups flour
1 tsp baking powder
½ tsp salt
1¼ cups chopped pecans

1 Pre-heat the oven to 350 degrees F.

2 Mix the butter and sugar together until creamy.

3 Add the dry ingredients and the nuts, and mix well.

4 Press the mixture into a greased 9 inch baking pan or a greased metal quiche dish.

5 Bake for 20 – 30 minutes until golden brown.

6 Cut into servings while still warm.

Makes: about 20 servings

Preparation time: 15 minutes

Index

Index by Page Number

SEAFOOD

Stuffed Trout 8
Thyme for Trout 9
Haddock with Mustard & Dill 10
Seafood Stir Fry 11
Spicy Shrimp 12
Fish Cakes 13
Herb Salmon with Cream Sauce 14
Mediterranean Seafood Kebabs 15
Scallop Kebabs 16
Herb Salmon Steak 17
Shrimp Toast 18
Crab Stuffed Salmon Wheels 19
Stuffed Orange Roughy 20
Red Snapper with Lime 21
Maple Mustard Glazed Salmon 22

POULTRY

Raspberry Chicken 24
Aromatic Chicken Skewers 25
Orange Ginger Chicken 26
Lime Butter Chicken 27
Spiced Chicken 28
Chicken with Sweet Orange 29
Chicken with Garlic, Lemon & Herbs 30
Chicken Strips 31

Indoor Grilling by Meriel Bradley :: www.MerielBradley.com

Chicken Wings	32
Whole Split Chicken	33
Chicken Fajitas	34
Rosemary Butter Stuffed Chicken Thighs	35
Turkey Burgers	36
Rosemary Lemon Chicken	37
Chicken Cordon Bleu	38
Chicken Kiev	39

BEEF

Ginger Beef	42
Spicy Marinated Steak	43
French Mustard Steaks	44
Orange Garlic Beef	45
Beef Stir Fry	46
Tacos	47
Beef Fajitas	48
Stuffed Steak	49
Steak with Asparagus, Onions & Mushrooms	50
Bacon London Broils	51
Steak in Red Wine Marinade	52
Steak & Brandy	53
Hamburgers	54
Steak & Pearl Onion Kebabs	55
Mixed Grill Kebab	56

Index by Page Number

PORK

Pork Kebabs 58
Pork, Sausage & Pepper Kebabs 59
Honey Pineapple Ham Steaks 60
Apricot Glazed Ham Steaks 61
Lemon Dill Pork Chops 62
Spicy Pork Chops 63
Port & Berry Chops 64
Sausage & Lemon Stuffing Burgers 65
Pork Ribs 66
Cumin-Yogurt Pork Chops 67
Pork Stuffed with Sage & Onion 68
Pork Stuffed with Onion & Apple 69
Pork Stuffed with Tomato & Rice 70

VEGETABLES

Spicy Potato Wedges 72
Mixed Vegetables with Ginger 73
Lemon Garlic Asparagus 74
Herby Eggplant 75
Vegetable Kebabs 76
Stuffed Mushrooms 77
Mediterranean Grilled Vegetables 78
Pea & Bean Stir Fry 79
Barbecue Onions 80
Red Potatoes 81

Indoor Grilling by Meriel Bradley :: www.MerielBradley.com

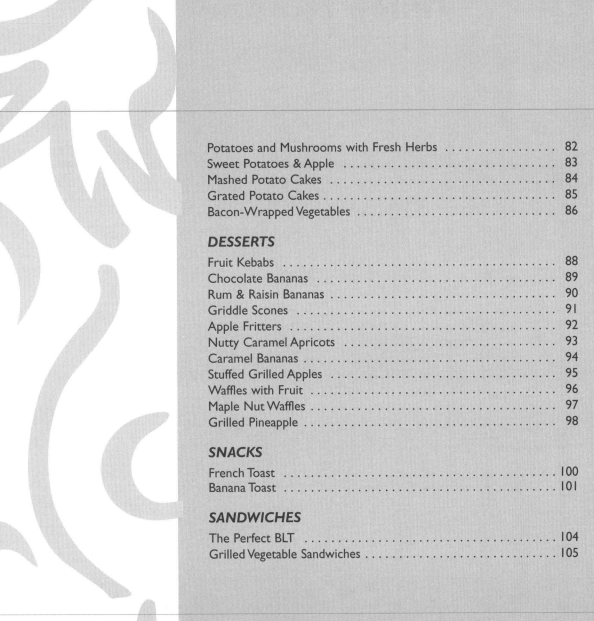

Potatoes and Mushrooms with Fresh Herbs 82
Sweet Potatoes & Apple 83
Mashed Potato Cakes 84
Grated Potato Cakes 85
Bacon-Wrapped Vegetables 86

DESSERTS

Fruit Kebabs 88
Chocolate Bananas 89
Rum & Raisin Bananas 90
Griddle Scones 91
Apple Fritters 92
Nutty Caramel Apricots 93
Caramel Bananas 94
Stuffed Grilled Apples 95
Waffles with Fruit 96
Maple Nut Waffles 97
Grilled Pineapple 98

SNACKS

French Toast 100
Banana Toast 101

SANDWICHES

The Perfect BLT 104
Grilled Vegetable Sandwiches 105

Index by Page Number

Pastrami & Swiss 106
Feta Cheese & Roasted Red Peppers 107
Smoked Salmon & Cheese 108
Chicken & Grilled Zucchini Wrap 109
Crab Meat & Grilled Zucchini Wrap 110
Beef and Grilled Mushroom & Onion Wrap 111
Portobello Mushroom Sandwich 112
Grilled Cheese & Tomato 113
Grilled Cheese, Ham & Onion 114
Grilled Pizza Cheese 115

DESSERTS
Banana Raisin Loaf 121
Strawberry Peach Crumble 122
Nutty Shortbread 123

Thoughts, comments & new recipe ideas

Thoughts, comments & new recipe ideas

Jot down your thoughts, comments & new recipe ideas and send them to Meriel at:

meriel@merielbradley.com

Serves: _____

Preparation time: _____

Thoughts, comments & new recipe ideas

Serves: _____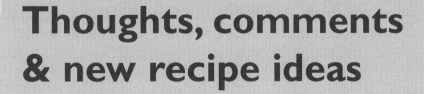

Preparation time: _____

Thoughts, comments & new recipe ideas

Jot down your thoughts, comments & new recipe ideas and send them to Meriel at:

meriel@merielbradley.com

Serves: _____

Preparation time: _____

Indoor Grilling by Meriel Bradley :: www.MerielBradley.com

Thoughts, comments & new recipe ideas

Serves: _____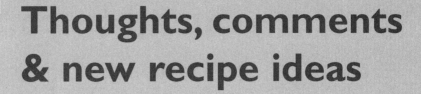

Preparation time: _____

Thoughts, comments & new recipe ideas

Jot down your thoughts, comments & new recipe ideas and send them to Meriel at:

meriel@merielbradley.com

Serves: _____

Preparation time: _____

Thoughts, comments & new recipe ideas

Serves: _____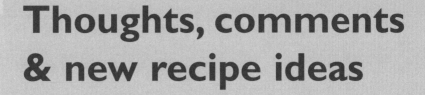

Preparation time: _____

Thoughts, comments & new recipe ideas

Jot down your thoughts, comments & new recipe ideas and send them to Meriel at:

meriel@merielbradley.com

Serves: _____

Preparation time: _____

Thoughts, comments & new recipe ideas

Serves: _____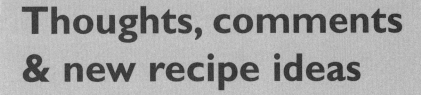

Preparation time: _____

Thoughts, comments & new recipe ideas

Jot down your thoughts, comments & new recipe ideas and send them to Meriel at:

meriel@merielbradley.com

Serves: _____

Preparation time: _____

Thoughts, comments & new recipe ideas

Serves: _____ |◉‖

Preparation time: _____ ↻

Thoughts, comments & new recipe ideas

Jot down your thoughts, comments & new recipe ideas and send them to Meriel at:

meriel@merielbradley.com

Serves: _____

Preparation time: _____